Chakras

A Comprehensive Manual On Utilizing Meditation To Achieve Chakra Balancing, Promote Physical Healing, And Enhance Positive Energy Levels

(Developing Knowledge Of Chakras And Utilizing The Practice Of Spiritual Healing Through Meditation)

Glenn Donnelly

TABLE OF CONTENT

Healing The Heart Chakra 1
Chakra Healing 8
The Advantages Of Balancing Your Chakras ... 15
Meditations For Balancing The Heart Chakra . 23
How Does Reiki Relate? 48
A Guide To Engaging With The Chakras 57
Sound-Based Chakra Therapy 63
Seven Yoga Asanas To Realign And Harmonize The Energy Centers Of The Body 65
Is There An Imbalance In Your Chakras? How To Know 87
Rejuvenating Oneself And Attaining A State Of Heightened Spiritual Vitality. 115
An Exposition On The Fundamentals Of The 7 Fundamental Chakras 119
Engaging In The Practice Of The Three Lower Chakras 137
Conclusion 144

Healing The Heart Chakra

The heart chakra, commonly known as the central chakra, is situated in the thoracic region near the anatomical location of the heart. It encompasses vital organs such as the heart, lungs, breasts, and the thymus gland, which holds significant prominence in both the lymphatic and endocrine systems.

As the title implies, it regulates one's cardiac function and the emotions associated with affection, empathy, and optimism. It is also associated with the process of spiritual enlightenment, fostering forgiveness, nurturing empathy, cultivating self-awareness, developing emotional intelligence, promoting inner peace, and enhancing one's capacity to embrace and engage with others on an emotional level.

What are the Consequences of a Blocked Heart Chakra and What are the Effects of an Open Heart Chakra?

When the heart chakra is unblocked, one experiences a pronounced sense of optimism concerning their capacity to bestow and accept affection, demonstrate self-compassion and empathy towards others, and successfully cultivate flourishing and harmonious connections with cherished individuals. Additionally, you possess a natural knack for acquiring profound self-awareness and engaging in extensive introspection to enhance your emotional intelligence. Your proficiency in effectively leading and pacifying individuals amidst a challenging circumstance is exemplary as well. Furthermore, your cardiovascular system and pertinent internal organs operate seamlessly.

Contrarily, when the heart chakra is obstructed, one experiences a diminished degree of self-awareness and emotional intelligence. You are inundated with profound sorrow, envy, indignation, animosity towards yourself and others, and possess a profound apprehension of experiencing betrayal. Furthermore, you experience a sense of restlessness and impatience, accompanied by irritability. Additionally, you encounter difficulty in placing trust in others and face a range of physical health issues such as elevated blood pressure, sleep disturbances, cardiovascular concerns, and a compromised immune system. To address these issues, it is recommended to incorporate the strategies expounded upon hereafter.

What are the techniques/methods for achieving balance in the heart chakra?

Presented herein are a collection of proven techniques aimed at reinstating equilibrium within the heart chakra:

Crystal Healing

It is advisable to incorporate green colored gemstones like Jade, Green Calcite, and Green Aventurine, as well as crystals associated with the heart, such as Rose Quartz, either in the form of jewelry or in their natural state, in order to facilitate the healing of your heart chakra. It would be advisable to don a pendant or necklace crafted from one of these stones, with a specific emphasis on Rose Quartz. Furthermore, ensuring that its length is sufficient to make contact with your heart chakra can effectively alleviate any discrepancies in its energy flow.

Meditative Practice

Please ensure that you are in a comfortable seated position. Take a few deliberate and deep inhalations and exhalations. Then, visualize a gentle and captivating emerald luminance enveloping your heart chakra. Gradually, allow this glowing energy to extend outwards, permeating your entire being, intensifying in both vibrancy and vitality with each passing second. With that being said, envision a removal of any form of negativity from your being, whilst being replenished solely with an influx of positivity.

Engage in this activity for a duration of 15 minutes every day, and you will promptly experience feelings of joy, empathy, and a deep affection towards both yourself and those around you.

Eat Healthy

Hot soups, various green foods like kale, green peppers, green apples, spinach, and limes combined with an assortment of vitamin C-rich foods such as citrus fruits and berries have profound effects on achieving equilibrium in your heart chakra.

Affirmations

Recite the subsequent affirmations, as well as any relevant ones, with a prominent smile on your face on a daily basis for a duration of 10 minutes in order to harmonize your heart chakra.

I am content and profoundly enamored with myself.

I exude a palpable aura of joy and affection wherever I happen to be.

I readily grant forgiveness to both myself and others.

I possess a profound understanding of my own identity and personal requirements, and I possess the capacity to meet them.

I am entirely receptive to extending and receiving additional love on a daily basis.

Furthermore, it is recommended that you engage in a morning walk in the fresh air during the early hours, when the levels of oxygen are at their peak, in order to maintain equilibrium in your heart chakra. Now, let us proceed to comprehend the fifth chakra.

Chakra Healing

As observed previously, chakras possess the propensity to become unbalanced and excessively active, exerting a profound influence on our physical well-being and overall state of being. Nevertheless, there are numerous approaches we can employ to address this matter and restore harmony to our chakras. Chakra healing pertains to the practice of consciously manipulating the energy flow within the various chakras encompassing the human body. Chakra healing can alternatively be described as chakra harmonization, as its objective is to restore the optimal alignment among the various energy centers.

"A harmonized chakra system, exemplifying optimal functionality, exhibits the following attributes:

The differentiation of the diverse frequencies and energies associated with each individual chakra.

Adequate alignment of polarity - reception and articulation.

Appropriate intensity.

Balance.

The optimal amount of energy present in each chakra.

Overall equilibrium.

Preferred orientation - in the counterclockwise or clockwise direction.

It is imperative to comprehend that the individual chakras cannot operate autonomously. Every single chakra forms an integral component of a interconnected array of energy centers comprising a comprehensive system. To gain a comprehensive understanding of the concept of chakra healing, one must acquire knowledge regarding the distinct functioning of each chakra and their interconnectedness. The aforementioned subjects were deliberated upon in the preceding section; hence, it is essential to ascertain one's possession of, or familiarity with, the knowledge imparted therein.

Our life experiences have a direct impact on the condition of our chakra. Every instance in our existence leads to the establishment of an energetic impression on our chakras, consequently influencing their functioning. As an illustration, our adverse encounters possess significant sway as they tend to prompt us to adopt defensive measures, leading to a subsequent constriction or repression of the energetic flow within the chakras.

This is the intended meaning behind our discourse on an obstruction in the chakra energy flow. When a chakra becomes obstructed, there is a considerable decrease in both the magnitude and the vitality of the energy that traverses through the chakras. The objective of chakra healing is to facilitate a harmonized circulation of energy throughout the entirety of our physique or within specific regions of the body. The provocation of our daily interactions, be it in the realm of emotions or through direct physical contact, induces a subtle electromagnetic shift within our body that manifests in our chakras. There is a variation in both the quality and the trajectory of energy channeled by each chakra, thereby leading to fluctuations in the overall equilibrium of the system.

The equilibrium of the chakra can also be influenced by our cultural milieu. An instance of such can be observed in cultures wherein the dominance of scientific methods, cognitive faculties, and rational thought leads to an inclination towards an exceedingly strong third eye chakra. The manner in which we live our lives extensively influences our chakras, particularly when we allocate time to establish a connection with the fundamental elements of the earth and harmonize ourselves with its inherent rhythm. For example, prolonged computer use and sedentary desk work can cause depletion of energy in the lower chakras, hindering essential grounding and impeding the flow of energy throughout the entire chakra system.

There exist numerous philosophical foundations that substantiate the practice of chakra healing, varying depending on the individual healer and their respective tradition. There exist, nonetheless, two prevailing theories which are widely acknowledged. Based on the initial source, it is evident that there exist two fundamental energy streams that significantly influence the equilibrium of the chakra system. A descending current originating from a pervasive and cosmic force, accompanied by an ascending current that arises from the terrestrial magnetic field and ascends towards the chakras. It is widely believed that these two primary channels of energy serve the purpose of restoring equilibrium to the entire system. An alternate proposition posits the significance of the ascendant energy flow originating from the root chakra and extending upwards.

This dichotomy in the energy's progression serves as a poignant reminder of the philosophical concept of "the power of the mind" and its influence on physical phenomena, in addition to the genesis and factors underlying the psyche. For the succeeding section of the chapter, our attention will be primarily directed towards the process by which energy traverses each chakra in order to restore equilibrium, with less emphasis on the philosophical underpinnings of the chakra theory.

The Advantages Of Balancing Your Chakras

If the alignment and balance of your chakras are achieved, you will experience the positive effects both externally and internally. You may also observe the impact in domestic, educational, professional, and various other settings. When one is in optimal health and wellbeing, they tend to experience contentment and cultivate a sense of trust and conviction. You will experience increased productivity and develop self-confidence.

It is imperative to periodically restore balance to your chakras, through a systematic examination of your life to identify any potential deficiencies. Once one develops the ability to detect a blocked chakra, they will consistently be vigilant in identifying any potential chakra imbalances, thereby ensuring optimal well-being.

Embracing oneself and cultivating inner assurance

Possessing well-balanced chakras will bestow upon you a profound sense of self-assurance, self-acknowledgment, and self-compassion. If one possesses self-assurance, the articulation of thoughts becomes effortless, fostering seamless communication with fellow individuals.

Self-acceptance comes from self-realization. This is accomplished by maintaining a state of equilibrium and wellness within the chakras. If one is able to achieve self-realization, they can effectively acknowledge their weaknesses and strengths, thereby eliminating any intimidation that may arise from their weaknesses. One can engage in refining them and subsequently transform them into a benefit.

Being granted the opportunity to tap into one's inherent wisdom

The cultivation of harmonious and well-aligned chakras facilitates a profound connection with a transcendent entity, enabling the realization and contemplation of one's innermost essence. Upon gaining comprehensive knowledge of oneself, one's level of self-awareness elevates, enabling a better understanding of personal weaknesses and strengths.

An advantage that you could avail yourself of involves tapping into your inherent wisdom, which will steer you towards leading a purposeful and significant existence.

Enhanced spiritual connection.

Upon successfully removing the blockage in your crown chakra, you will experience an enhanced interconnectedness with your transcendent source. Upon achieving an understanding of your Divine Source and cultivating a profound connection with them, you will gain the ability to effectively convey and relinquish all difficulties to your Divine Source, ultimately resulting in a state of tranquility.

Your crown chakra is the chakra that correlates with your spiritual dimension. If it achieves a state of equilibrium, it has the potential to facilitate substantial spiritual enlightenment. You will discover that achieving equilibrium between your yin and yang energies can be effortlessly attained. According to Osho, the renowned spiritual leader from India, one must find a way to exist within the confines of the world, yet remain detached from its influence.

More appropriate articulation

If an individual experiences a constrained throat chakra, it becomes challenging for them to communicate in a sincere manner. A single obstructed chakra can impede the harmonious circulation of energy throughout the remaining chakras, thereby exerting an influence over your entire system.

Having well-balanced chakras will facilitate the seamless articulation of your thoughts and emotions. This will lead to improved interpersonal connections, heightened happiness in one's existence, enhanced self-acknowledgment, and bolstered self-assurance.

Reduces anxiety and stress

When we have negative energy stored in our bodies, it could result in bad emotions like depression, anger, fear, anxiety, and stress. All of these have adverse effects on our health. The process of restoring balance to your chakras may entail the utilization of visualization techniques and engaging in meditative practices. This facilitates the process of unwinding and promoting relaxation, thereby mitigating the risk of developing symptoms associated with depression, anxiety, or stress.

Reduction in body mass

The presence of imbalanced chakras can result in adverse emotional states such as heightened stress levels and diminished self-confidence. These adverse sentiments can potentially contribute to an unhealthy lifestyle, subsequently leading to obesity and weight gain in numerous instances.

When the chakras are in a state of equilibrium and optimal well-being, they serve as a safeguard against the influence of these emotions, thereby diminishing the likelihood of leading an unhealthy lifestyle. An assortment of yoga postures possesses the ability to rectify obstructed chakras, facilitate unrestricted energy circulation throughout the entirety of the body, and contribute to the reduction of weight.

Improve your quality of sleep.

When an individual's chakras become obstructed, the flow of vital energy within the body becomes stagnant. This unfavorable energy can culminate in the development of insomnia. One can achieve optimal chakra healing through the practice of meditation. This approach represents the optimal solution for coping with insomnia. Engaging in meditation techniques correctly can facilitate easier sleep initiation, thereby promoting enhanced overall sleep quality.

Self-realization

Developing a state of optimal chakra health facilitates self-awareness and, in turn, provides insights into one's authentic life purpose. Once one gains a clear comprehension of the underlying motivations that give purpose to their existence, they will possess the ability to direct their attention towards matters of significance while diverting it away from trivialities that do not contribute meaningfully to their own life or the lives of others. Once you have a clear understanding of your true identity, you will be poised to experience the epitome of success and fulfillment in life.

Zeal for existence

When one is able to establish a connection with the spiritual domain, one can discern the genuine purpose and significance of existence. This will enhance your zest for life as you have evolved into a woman driven by purpose. Individuals who possess a clear understanding of their purpose in life display a fervent drive to pursue their objectives, in contrast to women who lack this sense of purpose. It transforms you into a woman who attracts the company of others and fosters an environment conducive to sharing their experiences.

Facilitating the release of negative energy through healthy means

When one's chakras are imbalanced, an excess of negative energy becomes present within. It is not imperative for the situation to remain as such, as the process of chakra healing possesses the potential to effectively eliminate any lingering negative emotions. Negative energy can materialize as adverse emotions, including feelings of shame, guilt, fear, and anger. When one achieves equilibrium in the rotation of their energy wheels, there will be an absence of any negative or stagnant energy confined within their being. It is purged in order to create space for an influx of positive energy.

This statement does not imply that life becomes less challenging. This implies that even during the most challenging times, you will not be exacerbating the difficulty upon yourself. To paraphrase a traditional proverb: 'The situation does not become simpler.' You continue to make progress."

Meditations For Balancing The Heart Chakra

A significant number of individuals approach the Heart Chakra with preconceived notions about its nature. A significant portion of our self-reflection is devoted to examining our innermost emotions and endeavoring to comprehend and interpret the communications conveyed by our hearts. As the fourth Chakra in our sequence, we are now ascending and nearing the uppermost part of our body. This is where we come to embrace sentiments such as affection and gain insight into the occasional discord between our rational thoughts and our emotional impulses.

Having an understanding of one's innermost being entails grasping their essence and delving into the depths of their being. It is by embracing the virtues of affection, empathy, and benevolence that lie within us that we can foster an environment conducive to offering and accepting love unreservedly. Let us delve into comprehensive knowledge regarding the Heart Chakra and explore the boundless depths of its inherent abundance.

What are the Characteristics Associated with the Heart Chakra?

The Heart Chakra is referred to as Anahata in Sanskrit, denoting the concept of being "Unstruck" or "Unhurt." This significant label facilitates comprehension that a well-operating heart is characterized by serenity, equilibrium, tranquility, and the absence of anxiety. Additionally, this term has the potential to signify "innocent" or "purified," alluding to the concept of a heart that is unencumbered and replete.

The Heart Chakra is situated precisely in accordance with its designation, within the vicinity of the cardiac region, albeit predominantly centered in the thoracic cavity instead of being laterally positioned towards the left. This ensures alignment with the rest of the Chakras, encompassing both those situated below and above it.

At this location, it engages with not just the heart, but also establishes contact with the spine, lungs, as well as various regions of the upper chest and upper back.

With regards to the physiological systems within the human body, it can be noted that the Heart Chakra is intricately linked to the Thymus Gland, which holds considerable significance within the Endocrine System. The Thymus Gland plays a pivotal role in overseeing the production of all hormones and maintaining optimal functionality of the immune system. Due to its positioning, the Heart Chakra is intricately interconnected with the cardiac and respiratory systems, affecting the well-being of both our physical heart and lungs. Given that the circulatory system maintains a direct correlation with the heart, it can be noted that the energetic influence of the Heart Chakra has the potential to exert an impact on various bodily components, owing to the uninterrupted flow of substances to and from the heart.

This can indicate complications pertaining to the extremities, namely the hands and feet, as well as difficulties related to the cranial region, lower extremities, and spinal region.

One might assume that the energy associated with the Heart Chakra would possess a red hue, as is commonly represented when depicting the heart. However, this belief would be inaccurate. The Heart Chakra is typically associated with the color green, as it is commonly utilized to evoke sentiments of vitality and well-being. Green also symbolizes monetary value, and it is the acquisition of riches and success that can be significantly impacted by the activation of this Chakra. Similar to the blossoming of plants in the Spring season, the color green is likewise linked to fresh advancements, an optimistic outlook towards what lies ahead, and a sense of anticipation and optimism for the future. It is a profoundly tranquil hue that carries connotations of rejuvenation and renewal, along with the restoration of spiritual vitality. The color green consistently beckons us to reconnect with the natural world, as wherever nature flourishes, so too does the concept of nurturing. This abode encompasses affection, vulnerability, ingenuity, perception, and hopefulness, in addition to benevolence and resolute ethical principles.

By immersing ourselves in the hue of green, we are expressing the notion that the present moment urges us to embark on a journey, unveiling a vast realm ready for us to embrace and radiate affection. By cultivating a harmonious state of the Heart Chakra, we can gain access to the full spectrum of benefits that are associated with the color green, and even go beyond those.

The Heart Chakra encompasses numerous affirmative attributes that naturally come to mind when contemplating an introspective exploration of an individual's innermost being. It is in this environment that we acquire the skills and knowledge to cultivate a life characterized by empathy and comprehension, enabling us to disseminate positivity among all we encounter. When the Heart Chakra is effectively activated, our existence becomes exceptionally gratifying as our core is imbued with affluence and serenity, frequently in generous amounts that enable us to distribute this prosperity. From this vantage point, you have the capacity to motivate and empower others to embrace a more wholesome existence while exemplifying unwavering love and encouragement to all. This does not imply that you permit others to exploit or mistreat you. Rather, it signifies that you possess a strong sense of self-worth and self-awareness, enabling you to assert yourself without compromising your personal security.

Our Heart Chakras afford us ample protection, and exude a gentle, nurturing warmth from deep within. It is imperative to frequently prioritize self-care and extend care towards others to ensure the fulfillment of your own needs and desires at all times. Maintaining one's mental, physical, and spiritual wellbeing is crucial in order to maintain an unobstructed and liberated state of the Heart Chakra.

The element conjoined with the Heart Chakra is air, a constituent recognized for its association with liberty and an unburdened disposition. Despite being imperceptible to the naked eye, it serves to amalgamate all the remaining elements, an attribute that applies equally to the Heart Chakra itself. In the very core of the chest, precisely aligned, the Chakras converge towards the Heart, establishing an interconnected system and distributing energies harmoniously throughout the body. Air provides the vital oxygen necessary for our respiratory system, enabling us to breathe, while also serving as a source of nourishment for our spiritual essence to thrive. Individuals who excel in the realm of the aerial element exhibit qualities of emancipation, resilience, and are imbued with whimsical notions. Air is an integral component of the natural world, and akin to the rhythmic pulses of our hearts that sustain life, its absence would precipitate cessation.

The Heart Chakra is symbolically depicted by a lotus blossom composed of a total of twelve delicate petals. Within, you shall discover a pair of triangles, one oriented in an upward direction whilst the other is directed downwards, converging harmoniously to produce a hexagram. The interlinked triangles symbolize the air element, as well as a wide range of contrasting concepts including but not limited to masculine and feminine energies. Despite the contrasting nature of these concepts, they are intricately linked to underscore the significance of connectivity to the Heart Chakra.

Recognition and Initiation
To discern the existence of your Heart Chakra, engage in a meditative practice wherein you concentrate on the region encompassing your chest. Direct your attention to all the various sensations that reside within this area. Your visualization should entail the manifestation of a vivid verdant glow

that radiates outward, enveloping your core and extending towards your dorsal region. With increased practice of this visualization technique, you will progressively enhance your ability to stimulate the expansion of that light, reaching every intricate part of your body and extending its influence outward.

When embarking upon the exploration of a particular Chakra, it is imperative to initiate the process by discerning the indications that manifest as a consequence of its disharmony. Several of the symptoms exhibit consistency across the various Chakras, for when there is an imbalance in one, it will invariably have an impact on several others. In the event that you detect the presence of various symptoms, it is highly probable that this is attributable to a disrupted flow of vital energy within your being. To rectify this situation, it is recommended that you proceed systematically by examining each individual Chakra, starting from the lowermost and progressing upwards.

A few indicators of a blocked Heart Chakra can encompass the presence of certain signs and symptoms:

- In intimate relationships, you experience significant jealousy and emotional turmoil.
- Trust is not inherent in your nature.
- Your tendency is to frequently exhibit defensiveness and withdrawal
- Behaviors characterized by a desire to please others and seek attention
- You exhibit a tendency towards being introverted and solitary
- Regrettably, you possess an incapacity to grant forgiveness and instead opt to harbor resentment.
- Your interpersonal relationships exhibit a significant degree of codependency.

- You lack self-perception of deserving love and refrain from expressing affection to others.
- You employ tactics of manipulation to achieve your desired outcomes " "
- You utilize strategic methods of influence to attain your objectives " "
- You employ cunning techniques to steer people and circumstances towards fulfilling your desires " "
- You demonstrate a propensity for manipulating individuals and events in order to achieve your goals "
- You seem to harbor a significant amount of animosity and rancor
- You lack interpersonal connections.
- You are experiencing conditions such as social anxiety and social phobia
- You possess a tendency to be self-critical and engage in self-depreciation.
- It appears that you have hypertension.
- It seems that you are afflicted with elevated blood pressure. ● It has been

determined that you have a case of high blood pressure. • It has been diagnosed that you suffer from hypertension. • Your medical condition indicates that you have high blood pressure.

• Certain respiratory ailments, like asthma, can affect one's breathing patterns.
• There is inadequate blood flow to the hands and feet
• Recurrent pulmonary infections like bronchitis

To initiate the process of addressing these illnesses, we can commence by nourishing our bodies with a diet abundant in essential nutrients. Every Chakra possesses a comprehensive selection of nourishing foods, and this holds true for the Heart Chakra as well. Prior to embarking on the cultivation of your mental and spiritual faculties, it is advisable to commence with aspects that are readily observable and within your sphere of control, such as exercising dominion over your dietary choices. This empowers you to foster a sense of self-assurance as you actively participate in nurturing your well-being, yielding tangible advantages for both your physical condition and the vitality of your Heart Chakra.

It is imperative to incorporate an abundance of verdant vegetables, such as spinach and kale, into your dietary regimen. In addition to their high iron and nutrient content, these possess a direct correlation with the Heart Chakra due to their profound verdant hue. Zucchini, broccoli, and Brussel sprouts are highly commendable green vegetables that merit frequent utilization in your culinary endeavors, alongside asparagus, peas, and even bok choy. Fruits serve as an additional commendable means of nourishing our bodies with energy. Apples, grapes, kiwis, cucumbers, and avocados are among the suggested fruit choices for promoting the optimization of the Heart Chakra. All of these food items possess the capacity to facilitate the maintenance of an optimal body weight and support the efficient functioning of the digestive system. In addition to the essentials, there exist several superfoods that possess remarkable benefits for our Heart Chakra, including matcha, green tea, chlorella, spirulina, and wheatgrass. Incorporate verdant herbs into your culinary preparations and salads, utilizing parsley, oregano, mint, coriander, basil, sage, and thyme. There are numerous culinary options available that can effectively enhance your chances of success. Hence, it is advisable to explore various recipes and commence the culinary process.

After nourishing yourself and attaining a state of mental preparedness, your subsequent task involves discerning the possible underlying factors responsible for the initial obstruction of your Heart Chakra. There exist numerous justifications, a few of which include:

- A diagnosis has been made indicating a significant medical condition
- You have recently relocated, either willingly or as a result of eviction.
- Your education has concluded, and you are now embarking on a professional career.
- You have recently concluded a significant romantic partnership.
- A beloved family member or dear friend has deceased
- There has been a solemn event in which a family member or close acquaintance has departed
- With deep regret, a cherished family member or trusted friend has left us
- There has been a deeply sorrowful occurrence involving the loss of a close family member or friend

- There are unresolved negative memories from your past
- There are unaddressed unpleasant memories from your past
- There are unresolved traumatic experiences in your past that you haven't confronted
- An increase or decrease in body weight has been observed in your case.
- You have been terminated from your employment

Regardless of the source of the obstruction, it is imperative that you ascertain its nature in order to surpass it. Consider allocating resources towards the acquisition of a personal journal, wherein you may diligently record your contemplations and reflections prior to retiring for the evening. This might incite you to delve into the depths of your innermost feelings, uncovering the underlying inhibitions that hinder you from experiencing love unconditionally.

The process of healing, achieving equilibrium, and sustaining

Having dedicated time to engage in journaling, you have successfully identified certain historical matters that might be impeding your progress. Additionally, through meditation, you have successfully pinpointed the existence of your Heart Chakra. Given these endeavors, what should be your subsequent course of action?

The subsequent phase in your expedition entails reconciling and restoring your inner being, thus achieving equilibrium and optimal well-being. We will examine five methodologies that have been demonstrated to be efficacious in addressing Chakras, thereby expediting your progression.

Contemplation and Mental imagery

To gain insight into your emotions, it is necessary to allow your heart the liberty to express itself candidly. Now, while that notion may appear peculiar, it is achievable through the practice of meditation. Identify a serene and tranquil setting conducive to meditation, preferably secluded from any possible disruptions. Please kindly shut your eyes and commence by deeply inhaling and exhaling at a relaxed pace, directing your full attention to each individual breath. As your physique enters a state of relaxation, you may initiate the process of redirecting your focus towards your inner self and actively engaging with your Heart Chakra. Within the confines of your thoracic cavity, the visual apparatus of your mind shall perceive a verdant lotus blossom engaged in a subtle, rhythmic circumvolution, or perhaps, a discernible but minimal sylvan fleck. Direct your attention towards the green light and inhale deeply, channeling your breath specifically towards it in order to foster its growth and expansion. As its development progresses, kindly prompt it to reveal the hidden truths it possesses. You may start to experience a sense of liberation as your heart communicates to your mind all the emotions and thoughts that have been accumulated. One might experience glimpses of past memories or resurface with prior emotions. Although being painful, refrain from suppressing your emotions and instead embrace them wholeheartedly. Engage in this practice on a daily basis until you experience a sense of alleviation and liberation within your heart.

Engage in Volunteer Activities

The heart serves as the focal point of inexhaustible and unqualified affection, and it is an offering that we ought to generously bestow upon those in our midst. To cultivate and enhance this aspect, engaging in volunteer work is certainly one of the most effective measures to undertake. Regardless of whether you derive satisfaction from engaging with children, animals, or volunteering at facilities such as a food bank, soup kitchen, or homeless shelter, there exist abundant prospects for you to actively participate and contribute. Initially, one may not experience a profound sense of generosity; however, upon encountering individuals who possess significantly fewer resources and opportunities, one will develop an enhanced gratitude for the abundance present in their own life. Engaging in acts of benevolence provides us with a sense of fulfillment, and it fosters personal growth by cultivating compassion and empathy within oneself. Even the most self-centered individuals can be persuaded toward altruistic endeavors by participating in volunteer activities. I urge you to access online resources to explore the range of opportunities currently accessible within your city or town.

Reciting a Mantra or Affirmation

The designated mantra affiliated with the Heart Chakra is Yam, to be vocalized by elongating the pronunciation of the "a" sound for approximately five seconds on each occasion.

During the practice of meditation, employing the Yam mantra can effectively center your attention and enhance the activation of your Heart Chakra. With each utterance, you will notice a gradual intensification of your emerald illumination, accompanied by a multitude of sensations coursing through your being.

In addition to the mantra "Yam," there exist alternative mantras capable of facilitating the healing of our hearts, including:

- Chattra Chakkra Vartee – A renowned mantra renowned for dispelling apprehensions and psychological barriers that hinder the realization of one's true potential.
- Guru Ram Das – This sacred incantation is employed to establish a profound link between your innermost emotions and that which surpasses one's individuality, enabling the illumination of ancient wisdom that has been transmitted across generations.
- Ra Ma Da Sa – In case one is confronted with profound emotional pain or unresolved past traumas, this mantra can be employed to facilitate genuine self-recovery. Additionally, it is possible to utilize this technique for exerting healing effects on others by mentally visualizing them while engaging in the act of chanting.

- Ong So Hung – This mantra is specifically intended to facilitate the expansion of your Heart Chakra and harmonize your spiritual essence and personal resonance with a transcendental force and heightened state of consciousness.
- Humee Hum Brahm Hum – This sacred chant serves as a conduit for our connection to a divine entity, serving as a gentle reminder that our essence is intertwined with a higher consciousness, resulting in the manifestation of our beautiful existence.

Furthermore, to augment the aforementioned mantras, one may employ daily affirmations as an ancillary method to fortify the desired virtues that are intended to be cultivated within the Heart Chakra. Recite this to yourself, whether vocally or mentally, numerous times throughout each day:

I am prepared to both give and receive love absolutely without conditions.
I possess the capability to genuinely grant myself and others forgiveness
- My Heart Chakra is receptive and potent.
- I opt to cultivate a sense of joy on a daily basis.
- I express sincere appreciation for the abundance I possess in my life.
- My decisions and choices are informed by love.
- I exclusively embrace relationships that are filled with affection and encouragement.

I deserve to receive love and respect." "• I am deserving of love and respect." "• It is appropriate for others to love and respect me.
- I possess a profound empathy for the well-being of all sentient beings
- I am currently engaged in the process of relinquishing all previous traumatic

experiences • My current efforts are focused on releasing all lingering effects of past traumas • I am actively working towards freeing myself from the burden of all past traumas • My current goal is to effectively disengage from any lingering effects of past traumas

How Does Reiki Relate?

A significant number of individuals have been exposed to the concept of "chakras" in conjunction with practices such as "Reiki" or "Reiki therapy." What precisely does this concept entail? This concept presents a level of intricacy that cannot be readily addressed with a simple solution or response. When individuals encounter this term, their initial association is often with an individual possessing the ability to affect healing through the use of their hands. However, this practice encompasses far more than solely that aspect. Essentially, the practice of Reiki healing involves rectifying disturbances in energy flow, alleviating stress, and fostering overall well-being in individuals.

An Approach to Facilitate Healing through Utilization of Energetic Frequencies:

Reiki is utilized to facilitate the restoration and harmonization of the energetic aspect encompassing both your physical being and spiritual essence. It is based on the assertion that there is a universal circulation of energy within all living entities in our world. Whenever there is an obstruction or disruption in the flow of this energy, it results in the manifestation of emotional disturbances and physical ailments. The objective of Reiki is to address this condition by harnessing the universal energy to establish a state of harmony and structure, leading to the restoration of health and well-being in the recipient of this therapeutic intervention.

On what premises does this practice rely?
Every therapeutic modality is predicated on certain premises, or underlying beliefs that serve as its foundation for

operation. "Presented below are several fundamental tenets of Reiki therapy and its potential for facilitating healing:

Connection: The core principle of Reiki healing revolves around the concept of a synchronizing energy force that interconnects all aspects of existence in our world. Despite the belief held by certain individuals that they exist in isolation from the broader world and universe, it is essential to note that such a notion is factually incorrect. This vitality permeates all aspects of existence, encompassing even the essence of your chakras.

Establishing Equilibrium: The modality of Reiki endeavors to identify zones where the emotional energy flow is impeded or obstructed. This impediment may manifest itself on physical, spiritual, psychological, or emotional levels, yet its impact is typically sensed across all of these domains.

Promotion of Positive Energy: The therapy of Reiki healing operates by reinstating equilibrium within the individual's energy, accomplished through the channeling of uplifting and constructive energy from the healer to the recipient, facilitated by the healer's hands. There is limited physical contact involved, and the actual level of physical activity during a typical session is minimal, similar to that of a massage session.

Concentration Ability: The Reiki practitioner possesses the capacity to concentrate their energy and direct it towards specific regions of the body in order to address any existing ailments, accomplished by applying their hands to the designated areas. They may also employ conventional stances for the purpose of achieving equilibrium and facilitating the activation of energy centers or chakras. While certain professionals refrain from physical contact with their clients, others will engage in direct tactile interaction by placing their hands upon you. During a healing session, it is possible that symbols associated with Reiki could be utilized, although this is not a definite occurrence.

Advantages of Reiki Therapy:
Reiki practitioners commonly employ supplementary treatment modalities, such as conventional medical interventions or therapeutic remedies. There are several benefits and advantages to be derived from this, namely:
Administration of Physiological Discomfort or Afflictions.

Comprehensive Restoration of Physical and Emotional Well-being.

Enhancement of Immune Functionality.

Enhanced Vibrational Resonance within the Human Physique.

The Origins of this Practice:
This particular method of healing was originated by a Japanese monk who, during his meditative sojourn in the mountains, stumbled upon its existence. While the credit for this finding is bestowed upon him, the existence of this omnipresent energy harnessed in Reiki predates the inception of our cosmos. His precise teachings enable individuals to harness and direct energy towards particular objectives. The procedure is instructed by an expert through a method known as attunement. Over the

course of time, these methodologies have undergone modifications and adjustments, ultimately resulting in the emergence of various branches of application. Nevertheless, all methodologies center their attention on the promotion of harmony and the restoration of overall well-being.

For whom is Reiki Healing appropriate?
Owing to the utilization of universally accessible energy, Reiki therapy offers benefits to individuals of all backgrounds. Many individuals undergo this form of healing alongside conventional medical treatments to address their physical ailments. Several hospitals have incorporated the use of Reiki practitioners to assist patients in their healing and recuperation, specifically targeting serious medical conditions. This particular form of healing can also prove advantageous to

the relatives or loved ones of the patient, who themselves may experience emotional depletion or fatigue alongside the patient. Below are several matters that Reiki has the capability to address:

Psychological Concerns: This encompasses conditions such as anxiety disorders, depressive symptoms, or even psychiatric disorders.

Mental Equilibrium: Encompassing difficulties in sustaining attention or maintaining orderliness in various aspects of one's daily routine.

Physical Conditions: Reiki healing has the potential to alleviate various physical ailments, including but not limited to, muscular contractions, chronic headaches, and other related issues.

The practice of Reiki healing serves as a means to address a multitude of concerns, encompassing the restoration and balancing of the chakras. Touch therapy can be beneficial for various animals, such as horses, felines, and canines. Reiki serves the purpose of restoring equilibrium and promoting mutual concordance within both human beings and animals, and possesses essentially boundless potential. If you are of the belief that this methodology possesses the potential to facilitate the restoration of equilibrium within your chakras, we would recommend conducting a diligent search for an accredited Reiki practitioner located within your vicinity.

A Guide To Engaging With The Chakras

WORKING WITH THE CHAKRAS

In the realm of chakra work, it is widely regarded as optimal to commence the process of opening chakras by starting with the lowermost chakra, specifically the root chakra, and progressively ascending through each subsequent chakra until reaching the crown chakra. Maintaining a state of awareness holds significant importance, as it facilitates the cultivation of self-awareness through the practice of meditation. This, in turn, promotes the harmonization of the chakras, which proves particularly beneficial when experiencing excessive chakra activity. The root chakra serves as the fundamental basis for all other chakras, and when it is open, individuals experience a sense of being embraced and secure. The ability to freely and confidently express one's sexuality and emotions occurs solely in an environment where one feels accepted and safe, aligning with the realm governed by the Sacral chakra. Sensations provide indications of personal desires, and with mindfulness one can activate the Manipura chakra to make deliberate determinations and assert one's aspirations. Assertion occurs within interpersonal and collective settings within society.

Once an individual develops the ability to effectively navigate social situations, they are likely to establish genuine and affectionate connections with others. This pertains to the realm of the Heart chakra, which subsequently helps mitigate any aggression or hostility originating from the throat chakra. Once interpersonal connections have been established, individuals may articulate their thoughts and ideas through the activation of the Throat chakra, thereby laying the groundwork for insightful thinking and the subsequent unlocking of the Third Eye chakra. Once all of these chakras have been opened, the individual becomes prepared to unlock the Crown chakra, thus cultivating self-awareness, heightened consciousness, and profound wisdom of the entirety.

Methods for Opening and Activating Blocked Chakras

When the flow of energy in the chakras becomes obstructed, it leads to disturbances in emotional, physical, and mental well-being, manifesting in symptoms such as impaired digestion, heightened anxiety, or persistent fatigue. A modest amount of guidance and instruction can facilitate the activation of chakras as an efficacious method of establishing a profound connection and orchestrating the flow of energy in the desired trajectory. In order to reinstate equilibrium within the chakras, individuals must attune themselves to their emotions first and subsequently determine which chakra to activate in order to counter any prevailing disharmony.

All of the seven chakras are intricately connected to nine distinct endocrine glands, as well as specific clusters of nerves referred to as plexus, thereby transforming them into integral components of the healing process. Each of your perceptions, potential states of consciousness, and sensory experiences can be divided into seven distinct categories, all of which can be related to specific chakras.

In the event that a specific area of your awareness experiences tension, consequently impacting the chakra associated with that particular area of consciousness, said tension is detected by the nerve of the plexus correlated with said chakra, subsequently transmitting signals to the portions of the energy and physical bodies regulated by said plexus.

If the prolonged duration or increased intensity of tension persists, it gives rise to physical symptoms necessitating the application of chakra healing for remediation. Once again, the manifestation of symptoms functions as a means of conveying to an individual, through the physical body, the conscious actions or thoughts taking place.

GUIDE TO CHAKRA HEALING

There exists a multitude of methods through which an individual can achieve equilibrium and restoration of their chakra, numbering in the thousands. It is achievable through the practices of visualization and meditation, which are widely favored options. Additionally, sound can serve as an alternative approach, and sight can be employed through the utilization of mandalas and yantras. Aromatherapy, known for its utilization of odors to facilitate the healing of chakras, proves to be highly effective as well.

Sound-Based Chakra Therapy

The practice of sound healing has been employed for millennia in diverse cultures spanning the globe. Through the provision of a consistent frequency, sound is capable of altering our brain waves. The synchronization of our brainwaves with sound leads to the subsequent harmonization of brain wave activity. Chakra Resonance refers to the phenomenon of a harmonizing effect taking place. Our chakras serve as energetic spheres that resonate, similar to the vibrations produced by sound. Utilizing musical notes for healing purposes proves to be a highly effective modality.

Before delving into the methodology of sound-based chakra healing, allow me to commence by acquainting you with the fundamental tones and their corresponding vowel counterparts:

Allow us to consider the initial chakra, known as the Root, by way of illustration. In order to restore balance to this energetic center, it is essential to utilize the fundamental frequency C and the phonetic representation "Uh." You must vocalize the keynote with the prescribed vowel sound.

Initially, engage in the process of mental imagery, directing your attention towards the depiction of your own self and fixating on the precise position of the Root, which is situated at the base of the spine. Observe the cyclical motion of the energy wheel and perceive its resonant vibrations. Additionally, please remember to mentally envision its hue, which is a vibrant shade of crimson red. Now, commence vocalizing the vowel 'Uh' in synchronization with the keynote 'C'. Ensure that it is gentle and softly done. Throughout the entire process, maintain focus on your primary chakra and envision a luminous red light. Please vocalize the "Uh" phoneme a total of 7 instances.

After finishing the Root chakra, proceed to the remaining energy centers. After the restoration of the seventh chakra, engage in a period of contemplative meditation while observing silence, followed by the intake of a profound breath.

Just like with the practice of meditation, ensure that you allocate a sufficient amount of time and obtain a suitable degree of privacy. Allocate some time to fully appreciate the rejuvenating effects of your healing experience and allow yourself to be revitalized by it.

Seven Yoga Asanas To Realign And Harmonize The Energy Centers Of The Body

One alternative manner to restore equilibrium and promote harmonious energy flow within the chakras is by engaging in various yoga postures. In the following chapter, we will explore seven exemplary yoga poses suitable for practicing in the comfort of your own residence. While it is possible to undertake these practices individually, depending on the specific chakra one aims to heal, it is strongly recommended to execute them in a sequential manner, proceeding from the base chakra to the crown chakra. During the pose, it is important to diligently concentrate on the inhalation and exhalation of your breath. Please be advised that if you have undergone surgery or sustained injuries recently, it is imperative to obtain medical clearance prior to engaging in yoga activities.

Root Chakra
Given that this chakra serves as the focal point for grounding, it becomes essential to employ a yoga posture that bolsters our capacity for establishing a firm

foundation. An example of such a stance is the Mountain Pose. To do this:

1. Assume a stance with your feet in close proximity, ensuring that your heels are modestly separated. If you encounter any challenges, you have the option to position your feet apart by a minimum of six inches or a greater distance. The majority of individuals are at ease with the hip-width area. Achieve a balanced weight distribution by raising your toes, widening them apart, and subsequently lowering them individually onto the floor.

2. Contract your quadriceps muscles while avoiding any strain on your abdominal region. Gently elevate your ankles, creating a cupped appearance with your feet. Achieve equilibrium by exerting inward pressure on the upper section of your thighs while simultaneously directing your pubis towards your navel.

3. Please maintain proper alignment and relaxation in your shoulder blades. Achieve this by applying slight pressure in the opposite direction, ensuring that your ribs remain aligned without protruding outward. Please position your arms to the rear.

4. Establish a conceptual axis extending from the apex of your cranium to the focal point of your pelvic region; employ such axis as a reference to preserve the equilibrium of your stance. Please ensure to maintain a state of relaxation for your head, as it is important that your chin remains parallel to the floor and not elevated.

Please sustain this position for approximately 30 seconds while maintaining a relaxed breathing rhythm.

Sacral Chakra

In order to facilitate unrestricted movement of energy within the sacral chakra, it is necessary to engage in specific exercises that target hip flexibility, such as the Wide-Stance Forward Bend. Please bear in mind that this posture serves as a source of energy for both pleasure and creativity, thus enabling a sense of well-being.

1. Commence by assuming a mountain pose, ensuring to take deep breaths in order to induce a state of relaxation in your physique.

2. Spread your feet apart. An alternative formal phrasing could be: "You may utilize your yoga mat as a reference point, ensuring that your feet are positioned in close proximity to the mat's perimeter.' To establish a stable foundation, apply strong pressure to the outer edges of your feet and firmly plant the balls of your big toes onto the floor.

3. Inhale deeply and once completely at ease, incline your upper body forward, ensuring that the impetus originates from the hip joints. As your upper torso achieves a state of being parallel to the

ground, proceed to apply pressure to your fingertips in a position that aligns directly underneath your shoulders. Take heed of your spinal alignment: it ought to be gently elongated, resulting in a subtle inward curvature from the base of the spine to the back of the neck region. Gently raise your neck upwards at a gradual pace.

4. While preserving the natural curvature of your spine, exert pressure upon the upper thighs in a rearward motion to facilitate the elongation of the torso. Inhale deeply, and proceed to insert your fingers between your feet while in a crawling position. Now, proceed to flex your elbows and gently lower your upper body, allowing it to elongate. If feasible, aim to rest the crown of your head on the floor to provide an additional source of support.

5. Gently move your fingers backwards until your forearms are at a right angle to the floor, and your upper arms are aligned in parallel. Please maintain this

posture for approximately 30 seconds to one minute, remembering to inhale deeply. Once the task is completed, assume a semi-erect position with your hands resting on your waist. Take a deep breath and rise fully. Return to the initial position.

Solar Plexus Chakra

In order to facilitate the activation and restoration of the Solar Plexus chakra, one may engage in the practice of Boat Pose or Full Boat Pose. Remarkably, it is pertinent to note that these postures also contribute to the well-being of the kidneys and intestines.

1. Commence by assuming a seated position on your mat, ensuring that your legs are fully elongated in front of you. Please position your hands at the side of your body, slightly to the rear of your hips. Extend your anterior torso by reclining slightly while avoiding excessive curvature of the spine.

2. Lower your knees and gradually elevate your legs from the ground, generating an angle of 45 to 50 degrees. At this juncture, your shins have already become parallel to the floor. Subsequently, elevate your arms laterally, ensuring they remain parallel to both the floor and your shins. Remember to actively involve your abdominal muscles, while avoiding excessive thickness and rigidity. Your chin ought to be directed towards your sternum. Ensure that your chin is aligned with your sternum. It is important to position your chin towards your sternum. If possible, please consider elevating your legs fully, positioning your feet above the level of your eyes. Engaging in this activity will result in the formation of a V-shaped contour by your body. This posture is known as the full boat pose.

3. Remain in this posture for a duration of 10 seconds, and extend it to 20 seconds should you find it manageable.

Once you have developed a significant level of proficiency with this posture, you will be capable of maintaining it for a duration of one minute.

This specific posture can be quite fatiguing. Should you encounter any difficulty, it is advisable to pause momentarily and revert to the previous step until you attain a sufficient level of comfort.

Heart Chakra

The yoga asana corresponding to the fourth chakra holds symbolic significance as it represents the focal point of energy associated with love, compassion, and acceptance. The most effective approach to facilitate healing is to expand our perspective and engage with the world in which we are intricately interconnected. An exemplary illustration of a pose that promotes openness of the heart is the Cow Pose.

1. Commence by assuming a "tabletop" position, wherein you position yourself on your hands and knees with your spine aligned in an upright but relaxed manner. It is of importance to ensure that your knees are positioned beneath your hips, while your shoulders, elbows, and wrists align in a perpendicular manner with the floor. It is important to ensure that your head remains free of tension. Please relax your head into a neutral position, with your gaze directed towards the floor.

2. Take a deep breath, while concurrently elevating your chest and sitting bones upward, lowering your abdomen towards the floor, and simultaneously raising your head. Experience the sensation of your chest being elongated - this is the primary purpose behind designating this pose for the 4th chakra.

3. Exhale and Inhale. Please perform the action for a complete duration of one minute.

Throat Chakra

To attain equilibrium or facilitate the restoration of the throat chakra, it is necessary to engage in neck area elongation. In this context, the Fish Pose serves as a highly beneficial physical activity.

1. Assume a supine position, with your knees flexed and your feet resting parallelly on the floor, while keeping your hands positioned by your sides. Take a deep breath while simultaneously raising your hips slightly and positioning your hands under them. Bring your pelvis down. At this juncture, your posterior is resting on the posterior part of your hands. Ensure that you maintain a compact position by keeping your arms in proximity to your sides.

2. Take a deep breath, followed by exerting pressure on the floor using your elbows and forearms in order to obtain leverage. Elevate your upper body and

raise your head from the ground. Subsequently, relinquish control of your head and proceed to reposition it onto the surface. Based on the curvature you have created, either the posterior region of your head or the pinnacle would be in contact. Currently, your neck is extended, but it is important to ensure that it is not subjected to excessive force, as we must avoid straining it.

3. Maintain the current stance for a duration of 20 to 30 seconds, ensuring a steady and controlled breath throughout. Breathe out and lower your upper body to the ground. Repeat for 1 minute.

Third Eye Chakra

As previously indicated, meditation represents the most efficacious means by which to restore or activate the Third Eye chakra, as it attends to our intellect and perception. Nevertheless, should one desire to integrate meditation practices with yoga, the optimal choice would be to engage in the Hero Pose.

1. Assume a kneeling posture and gradually lower yourself onto your calves. If you experience discomfort, you have the option of positioning a small pillow or rolled towel between your thighs and calves. Assume a stance wherein your feet are set apart wider than the breadth of your hips, while maintaining contact between the inner sides of your knees. Currently, you are situated in a seated position, with your feet positioned in close proximity.

2. Please position your hands on your lap, ensuring that your palms are facing downward. Inhale and exhale gently while sustaining the posture for approximately 30 seconds to 1 minute.

This particular posture is particularly beneficial if one is experiencing headaches, as they can be indicative of an obstruction in the second chakra.

Crown Chakra

If one desires to attain mental clarity and access profound insights, the Tree Pose represents an ideal choice.

1. Commence the exercise in a mountain pose, subsequently gradually transferring a greater proportion of your body weight onto the left foot, ensuring a firm placement of the outer side upon the floor. Elevate your right knee and secure your right ankle using your right hand.

2. Please apply pressure to your right foot against the inner part of your left thigh. If it is within your capacity, please endeavor to depict the scenario wherein the ball of the right foot comes into contact with the region in the vicinity of the groin. Keep the toes pointed.

3. Position your hands on your pelvis and subsequently, when you have established comfort, elevate them to your chest in a reverent stance. Maintain

that posture for a brief duration prior to lowering your hands and elevating them forcefully above your head.

4. To assist you in maintaining your equilibrium, direct your focus towards a stationary entity. Maintain this posture for a duration of 30 seconds to 1 minute prior to delicately lowering your foot and hands. Perform the task in a similar manner on the opposite side.

The Crown Chakra

The final Chakra that requires your attention is none other than the Crown Chakra. The donning of the Crown conveys wisdom and authority upon its wearer. This Chakra similarly responds to the collective consciousness and wisdom in the same manner. To provide greater clarity, this Chakra symbolizes the establishment of a profound link with the spiritual realm and the transcendent entities that govern our being, subsequently disseminating their influence in our surrounding environment. It portrays the transcendent bond that surpasses conscious awareness, enlightening individuals to the essence of their spiritual energy. Specifically, it assists in attaining a meaningful existence, liberating oneself from personal confinement or complacency, and unveiling the practice of mindfulness.

Nevertheless, an imbalance in the Crown Chakra can give rise to a spiritual disharmony within your being, resulting in the hindrance of energy flow from the Chakra situated beneath it, namely the Third Eye Chakra. The Crown Chakra can be understood as a pivotal repository of collective consciousness, integrative both intellectual and spiritual realms. Consciousness may alternatively be denoted as the faculty of the intellect. This phenomenon arises from the inherent capacity to yield profound positive or negative effects, contingent upon one's level of consciousness or degree of awareness. Consequently, it has the potential to either lead to success or failure. This is the condition that arises when one's awareness is heightened - it operates to one's advantage by adhering to one's unrestrained disposition in a regulated manner. It facilitates the establishment of a connection between one's subconscious mind and the elevated state of consciousness through the creation of a transcendent bridge. Furthermore, it assumes a significant role in facilitating your cognitive processes.

Hence, when your faculties of awareness are disciplined to align with proper conduct, it is probable that you will attain affluence and accomplishment in your existence. Naturally, the robust crown Chakra facilitates an individual's ability to embrace life's fluctuations with a positive and assured mindset. Moreover, it enables individuals to excel and exert a constructive influence on their surroundings.

The Characteristics of the Crown Chakra

Site: Positioned at the cranial apex, the Crown Chakra resides within the frontal region of the head, specifically atop the forehead.

Color Element: This entity exhibits an affinity towards the hue ultraviolet, occasionally manifesting in shades of purple, white, or gold.

Sangkrit: It is referred to as Sahasrana in the Sangkrit language.

Fundament & Obligation: The fundamental aspect of the Crown Chakra pertains to spirituality. It corresponds to the interplay of the elevated state of consciousness and the inherent cosmic essence contained within the human physiological framework. It also signifies the invocation of divine grace, illumination, and most notably, establishing a profound connection with the inherent force of Universal energy. The paramount energy that sustains the entirety of our planet, Earth, is the universal energy, and one of the fundamental constituents of Earth is humankind.

The yoga posture associated with the Crown Chakra is the headstand, which may appear unconventional. It is the position to support the flow of blood to your brain like when you find yourself empty at the head; that is when your brain lacks blood. The designated location for this Chakra involves positioning your hands in a manner where they are placed in front of your abdominal region, with the fingers interlocked and the pinky fingers oriented upwards.

The attainment of equilibrium in the Crown Chakra can be accomplished through a process that hinges upon the state of both mindfulness and cognizance. It entails acquiring a deeper comprehension or awareness of one's own aspirations and ambitions in order to fulfill them. Furthermore, possessing sagacity and a resolute mentality entails envisioning the repercussions of one's decisions and adeptly navigating through any ensuing ramifications.

Conversely, in the event of an obstruction in the Crown Chakra, individuals may experience a pervasive sense of encountering difficulties in their endeavors, regardless of their location. Issues arise as a consequence of your choices, challenges ensue, particularly as a result of shortcomings in your psychological and critical thinking abilities.

In the event of hyperactivity in the Crown Chakra, individuals may experience an excessive preoccupation with matters pertaining to the spiritual realm, thereby exhibiting signs of compromised discernment or uncertainty in decision-making.

It is a straightforward task to soothe the hyperactive Crown Chakra and restore equilibrium to it. Simply remain in a state of tranquility and quietude. It can be accomplished by engaging in meditation practices or by adopting a state of serene contemplation. Certain individuals may encounter difficulty in accomplishing this task; nevertheless, upon successful completion, one will attain a state of tranquility and experience an expansion of their awareness. It is imperative that you cultivate mastery of this Chakra by exercising restraint and refraining from allowing it to govern your actions. It is imperative to maintain a firm grasp on reality and exhibit composure and self-control. This is indicative of the exemplary leadership displayed by a discerning monarch over his realm. This is the proven strategy that enables warriors to emerge victorious in battles. This methodology can also be employed to reach appropriate decisions in one's personal life. It is essential to be cognizant of the moments when one must engage in thoughtful contemplation and deliberate action, as well as recognize instances when it is prudent to exercise patience, maintain composure, and seek mental clarity.

The hue associated with this Chakra is violet; immerse yourself within its chromatic embrace. One may experience a greater sense of ease if they happen to possess an affinity towards the color purple. Furthermore, it is noteworthy that the functionality of your Crown Chakra also impacts your rest and work. It is necessary for us to ascertain the appropriate time to take rest and to engage in activity.

In the event of excessive activation of the Crown Chakra, your mental and physical faculties may enter a state of hyperactivity, potentially leading to a state of exhaustion. It is of utmost importance to consistently bear in mind the necessity of avoiding excessive workloads. In terms of enhancing this Chakra, viable options for consumption may include purple potatoes, grapes, beets, and eggplants. They play a crucial role in the cultivation and enhancement of the energy within the Crown Chakra, ensuring the maintenance of a robust and resilient state of consciousness.

Is There An Imbalance In Your Chakras? How To Know

It is highly probable that if you have compiled a roster of adverse emotions, your chakras are unequivocally lacking equilibrium. This is due to the fact that experiencing repetitive negative emotions can lead to an imbalance in your chakras. Within the following chapter, we shall delve into the correlation between the aforementioned emotions and the seven chakras residing within your being. Additionally, we will explore the concomitant afflictions of physical pain and disturbances that arise as a consequence of this state of imbalance.

The Root Chakra

The initial chakra is conceivably the most straightforward to experience an imbalance. It addresses fundamental necessities such as shelter, access to clean water, financial security, and sustenance. As a result of this, emotions such as fear derive their foundation from the root chakra. The apprehension of job insecurity, the worry of being unable to meet mortgage or rental obligations, both exert an impact on the fundamental energy center known as the root chakra. If an individual has experienced trauma that is associated with feelings of abandonment or the loss of a cherished friend or family member, it is possible that such traumatic experiences could hinder the optimal functioning of this particular energy center.

In the event of a blockage in your root chakra, you might experience heightened sensations of fear and insecurity. You will adamantly refuse to embrace change. Anxiety likewise pertains to this classification, particularly when it manifests as uncontrollable or disproportionately excessive in relation to the circumstances. One may seek to establish their sense of identity by adhering to tradition or embracing their cultural background. One might inadvertently develop a desire for nourishing or soothing food options such as hearty stews and root vegetables that originate from the ground. One may experience profound feelings of insecurity within interpersonal connections or display symptoms of depression. Exhibiting a lack of energy or motivation is indicative of an obstructed root chakra, as well as an inclination towards seclusion and detachment from the outside world (which may also manifest during episodes of depression). If an individual's root chakra is significantly impacted, their behavioral response may manifest as withdrawal and negligence, reaching a level where they are unable to secure employment or meet their rental obligations. The very manifestations of our fears become evident when we fail to exert the necessary diligence in the process of chakra healing. In the eventuality of the most unfavorable outcome, the individual becomes entirely withdrawn and presents substantial difficulties in terms of accessibility.

Manifestations of a hindered root chakra encompass ailments pertaining to blood circulation, urinary or anal infections, bowel irregularities, and diminished libido. Females may experience a complete lack of inclination, while males may suffer from erectile dysfunction. Individuals afflicted with an obstructed root chakra may likewise encounter symptoms such as persistent chronic fatigue syndrome or undesired weight amplification. Individuals experiencing this obstruction may exhibit signs of addiction, as they experience an intense yearning for regularity and familiarity.

Should your root chakra exhibit excessive activity, it is likely that you will be more prone to experiencing anger readily. One may exhibit tendencies of aggression, resulting in the alienation of individuals who should ideally serve as their support network, or they may display possessiveness and attempt to exert excessive control over others. One might potentially experience detrimental engagement in sexual activities, such as excessive reliance on it for emotional solace or engaging in partner mistreatment. You could be perceived as parsimonious and lacking in magnanimity when it comes to your finances.

Manifestations of an excessively stimulated root chakra encompass indicators such as feelings of restlessness, sporadic facial or leg contractions, and a heightened libido beyond normal bounds. Instances of irritable bowel syndrome, bouts of diarrhea, and urinary tract infections may also manifest as a result of an excessively active root chakra.

The Sacral Chakra

The sacral chakra plays a crucial role in maintaining equilibrium between your sexual experiences and artistic expression. If you experience feelings of anxiousness or a sense of social detachment, it is possible that these emotions are originating from your sacral chakra. If you have experienced mistreatment and continue to feel its impact, it is possible that this energetic center has become impaired as a result.

In the event of an obstruction within your sacral chakra, you might encounter sensations of remorse, diminished self-value, and an intensified inclination towards prioritizing the satisfaction of others over your own. You may experience a diminishment in your creative abilities and demonstrate heightened sensitivity, thereby being more prone to emotional distress at a rapid pace. You may experience a sense of inadequacy and isolation, as though you are unable to elicit the interest of others. You will experience social isolation, rendering you unable to cultivate meaningful relationships, thereby causing distress within the relationships you can maintain. You are likely to experience a diminished sense of self-worth and adopt a negative outlook. In general, your performance will exhibit a lack of enthusiasm and motivation, accompanied by a lack of direction and a timid disposition.

Manifestations of an obstructed sacral chakra encompass diminished libido, discomfort in the lumbar region, ailments affecting the spleen, pancreas, kidneys, or reproductive organs. Women who have blockages in their sacral chakras may suffer from abnormal menstruation patterns. Both males and females can encounter fertility complications and engage in binge-eating disorder. One may experience a decreased libido or diminished sexual desire, as well as noticeable weight loss.

Should your sacral chakra exhibit signs of excessive activity, you might experience feelings of hypersexualization or engage in compulsive sexual behaviors. Furthermore, individuals may engage in the manipulation of sexual energy and employ sexual encounters as a means to exert control over their relationships, a profoundly perilous undertaking. It is possible that you harbor a sense of pride or arrogance, and perceive yourself as being superior to others. It is possible that establishing connections with individuals may prove challenging for you due to your tendency to hold a condescending attitude towards them. It is possible that you might experience symptoms of love addiction, leading to the development of codependent and unhealthy relationships characterized by jealousy and difficulties in establishing boundaries.

Physical manifestations encompass heightened sexual drive or an increase in body mass. You may experience the growth of cysts in the ovaries and encounter complications affecting the kidneys, pancreas, spleen, and reproductive organs. Painful urination or excessive urination, as well as the acquisition of sexually transmitted diseases, are also probable.

The Warrior Chakra

The warrior chakra governs the sense of identity and capacity to accomplish personal objectives, transforming aspirations into decisive actions and accomplishments. Experiencing an abusive relationship can have adverse impacts on your warrior chakra, as well as impede your functioning in various settings such as work and school.

Should your warrior chakra be obstructed, you may experience symptoms encompassing a sense of insignificance, diminished self-worth, and a noticeable incapacity to initiate action. One might experience a sense of inadequacy and be burdened by the perceived futility of one's aspirations. One may face limitations in managing fundamental aspects of one's life, as well as encountering codependency within interpersonal dynamics. It is possible that you are afflicted with an eating disorder and exhibit a low body weight.

Manifestations of an obstructed warrior chakra encompass variations in body mass, the onset of diabetes, conditions of inadequate or excessive blood sugar levels, as well as the emergence of obsessive-compulsive disorder and acute anxiety. Asthma, bronchitis, along with a myriad of respiratory ailments, can ensue, in addition to arthritis and afflictions affecting the liver and kidneys. In individuals with an obstructed warrior chakra, there is a potential manifestation of fibromyalgia and neural discomfort, alongside digestive complications affecting the small and large intestines, as well as anorexic tendencies.

In the event that your warrior chakra is excessively stimulated, you may experience a heightened sense of competition with those around you, which may result in a lack of harmony or wellness. Consequentially, you might find yourself inclined to display ostentatious behavior or exhibit an excessive need for control within your interpersonal relationships.

The physiological manifestations of an excessively stimulated warrior chakra encompass the experience of engaging in compulsive consumption patterns leading to the development of an eating disorder and subsequent weight gain. One may potentially develop gastric ulcers in addition to experiencing issues related to excessive exertion or physical fatigue.

The Heart Chakra

Given that the heart chakra is closely associated with matters of romantic relationships, it is worth emphasizing that instances of abuse within such relationships or any form of sexual abuse can have a profound impact on this particular chakra. If you are confronted with numerous challenges in your romantic relationships or encounter difficulties in fostering creativity, it is plausible that you are experiencing an inherent discrepancy in this aspect.

If an obstruction occurs in the heart chakra, individuals may experience a heightened sense of social exclusion and emotional detachment. One may experience profound solitude and overwhelming apprehension regarding the potential loss of existing connections. You might find it challenging to express your authentic self freely or to genuinely connect with another person's true essence. One's dispositional tendencies may include harboring resentments, exhibiting feelings of envy, and demonstrating insecurity within interpersonal connections. Your ability to articulate yourself will be hampered and you will experience a sense of creative deficiency. You might tend to be excessively judgmental.

Physical manifestations encompass inadequate circulation of the blood, malignancies affecting the breasts or lungs, or complications within these anatomical regions. Discomfort experienced in the region of the upper back and shoulders, along with muscular soreness and respiratory conditions such as asthma.

If one is experiencing an excessive activation of the heart chakra, it may hinder their ability to establish suitable boundaries within interpersonal connections. It is possible that you are experiencing symptoms of codependency and grappling with challenges related to personal identity. One may develop a dependence and experience love addiction, enduring abusive relationships due to the apprehension of being alone.

Pulmonary ailments such as cancer and emphysema are among the observable manifestations of an excessively activated heart chakra. Elevated blood pressure is an indication of an excessively stimulated cardiac chakra. You may also experience cardiac issues such as murmurs, palpitations, and potentially be prone to myocardial infarctions.

The Throat Chakra

The throat chakra pertains to the highest level of reality. If one struggles with maintaining inner and interpersonal honesty, this particular chakra possesses the potential to exert a significant influence. If an individual possesses trust-related concerns or has experienced betrayal within a romantic partnership, it is possible that this particular chakra may manifest an imbalance.
Should you encounter obstructions in your throat chakra, it will impede your capacity to articulate your thoughts and

emotions. You might possess a clear understanding of your personal desires, yet face difficulty in manifesting them in your concrete existence. This implies that you will be deprived of the ability to establish effective communication within your interpersonal connections or articulate your emotions to others. You might experience anxiety when it comes to addressing a large audience or alternatively, demonstrate excessive reticence. This can result in heightened levels of anxiety during social interactions and subsequent feelings of social isolation.

The manifestation of a compromised throat chakra may present itself in bodily symptoms such as tongue and mouth disorders including tumors and ulcers, thyroid dysregulation resulting in the hypofunctioning of the thyroid gland, vocal discomfort and huskiness, cephalalgia, dental issues, and discomfort in the neck and jaw region.

Should an excessive surge of energy manifest in your throat chakra, it is plausible that one might engage in excessive or untimely discourse. One might misinterpret social cues and exhibit impulsive behavior, resulting in verbalizing inappropriate or discomforting remarks for others. You may have a strong desire for attention and resort to inappropriate methods to attain it. You may exhibit unkind and excessively critical behavior towards others and towards yourself. One might experience a sense of detachment from the transcendental.

The overactivity of the throat chakra can manifest in various physical symptoms, such as recurrent occurrences of colds, strep throat, laryngitis, persistent earaches or ear infections, as well as discomfort in the neck region.

The Chakra of the Third Eye

The third eye chakra pertains to the faculties of clear perception, discernment, and authentic self-awareness. If one experiences a sense of being directionless in life, it is conceivable that there might be disturbances associated with this particular chakra. An obstruction in this area will have significant implications and potentially result in the development of severe psychiatric disorders such as schizophrenia and intellectual disability.

In the event that there is an obstruction within the third eye chakra, an individual may experience a sense of directionlessness or lack of purpose in their life. You will experience difficulties in maintaining concentration, exhibit limited self-control, manifest a sense of apprehension towards others, and encounter varying degrees of paranoia. This situation may intensify over time, culminating in heightened levels of paranoia. It is possible that you may start experiencing hallucinations, false beliefs, or symptoms consistent with paranoid schizophrenia.

Manifestations of an obstructed third eye chakra may encompass various neurological ailments, persistent fatigue, and attention deficit hyperactivity disorder. Furthermore, conditions such as headaches, migraines, myopia, and various ocular disorders may also ensue. The propensity for seizures or stroke can be significantly enhanced in the presence of a blocked state of this chakra.

If an abundance of energy is present in the third eye chakra, it may manifest as a sense of arrogance. Overly focused on professional advancement at the expense of others, lacking awareness of the impact of your actions on others. In interpersonal dynamics, especially when holding a position of authority, one may exhibit behaviors indicative of being highly manipulative and authoritarian. An individual who devotes an excessive amount of energy to their third eye chakra may exhibit a high level of religiosity and resolute adherence to their belief system. One might experience symptoms of paranoia and exhibit delusional thinking and hallucinations.

The physical manifestations of an abundance of energy in this chakra typically include insomnia, migraines, distressing dreams, and ear discomfort. Complications may arise involving the ocular and cerebral regions, alongside issues affecting the sinuses.

The Crown Chakra

This particular chakra facilitates the connection between oneself and the realm of spiritual illumination and guidance. When the pathway is obstructed, one's access to truth and divine counsel will be severed, inevitably triggering profound emotional anguish that can potentially manifest in a multitude of ways.

If one's crown chakra becomes obstructed, there may arise a sense of estrangement from one's colleagues, peers, and a diminished sense of connection to the spiritual realm. This can result in profound solitude and detachment from society, rendering the attainment of one's objectives unattainable. In the presence of a severe and unaddressed obstruction, there is a possibility of losing sight of one's objectives.

Manifestations of an obstructed crown chakra encompass psychiatric conditions such as schizophrenia, paranoid ideation, Alzheimer's disease, Parkinson's disease, and depressive disorders. It is possible that you are experiencing migraines, insomnia, sleep apnea, and neurological disorders. Brain diseases, such as cancer, can also manifest.

In the event that your crown chakra experiences excessive activation, you may perceive a sense of disconnection from the surrounding environment. One's reliability may diminish as they begin to neglect their own and others' needs within their interpersonal connections. You run the risk of experiencing a diminished capacity for empathy, along with a corresponding decrease in your inclination to engage in empathetic behavior. It is possible that you are experiencing symptoms of depression. One might experience feelings of envy, inadequacy, or resentment.

Manifestations of an excessively stimulated crown chakra can be observed through indicators such as vertigo, a sense of disorientation, or cognitive haziness and perplexity resulting in inadvertent bodily accidents. Both seizures and heightened sensitivity to light are frequently encountered.

When the equilibrium and optimal functioning of your chakras are achieved, you will experience noticeable sensations. You will effectively address challenges using constructive methods, resulting in a sense of well-being, vitality, and spiritual harmony. Nevertheless, it is highly likely that one does not constantly experience a state of perfection, and it is a prevalent occurrence in our society to encounter an imbalance in chakras. One is likely to experience a sense of being unbalanced or disoriented in any of the aforementioned manners. By attaining alignment between mental, physical, and spiritual indications, it is possible to discern which aspects are in a state of disharmony.

When determining the imbalance of chakras, it is generally prudent to assume that there are multiple affected. They are all inextricably interconnected, and any obstruction in one will inevitably lead to complications in the rest. This assertion applies particularly to the root chakra and the crown chakra, necessitating diligent attention to the well-being of these two chakras. They serve as the primary and ultimate conduits, possessing the greatest degree of connectivity to the external environment and susceptibility to obstruction. Exercise caution in monitoring the state of your heart chakra, as it possesses a significant capacity to become obstructed due to its role in connecting the spiritual and physical chakras.

After compiling your list, you will gain clarity regarding your emotions. This tool enables individuals to perform self-diagnosis and ascertain the specific chakras that may be impacted, drawing from their emotional and mental condition. Nevertheless, it is worth noting that there is considerable overlap among several mental symptoms, hence it is essential to take notice of the specific location where physical pain is experienced. It is advisable to adhere to the practice of attentively attending to the signals of your body and discerning the precise locations where your pain and unease manifest.

In the event that you experience apprehension regarding job stability, recurrent urinary tract infections, and/or discomfort in the legs, it is likely indicative of an imbalance in the root chakra. If you happen to possess an imbalance in the root chakra, it is highly probable that there exists a corresponding imbalance in the remaining chakras.

Determining and pinpointing specific ailments associated with precise chakras often poses considerable challenges, and in certain instances, despite one's perusal of the provided information, the identification of blocked or excessively stimulated chakras might remain elusive. Do not worry, as you will still have the ability to achieve equilibrium through the deliberate cultivation of mindfulness and dietary habits. Generally, one can ascertain the primary chakras accountable for their difficulties, aiding in their self-improvement. Nevertheless, even in instances where such identification proves challenging, individuals can still make positive strides towards their own betterment.

Rejuvenating Oneself And Attaining A State Of Heightened Spiritual Vitality.

Do not allow yourself to be disheartened if, upon your initial attempt at meditation, you do not perceive the anticipated spiritual metamorphosis. Similar to any newly acquired skill, meditation requires practice. There exist certain actions that can be implemented in one's daily routine to enhance concentration abilities. When confronted with routine and mundane tasks, endeavor to adopt a fresh perspective and approach. Please refrain from expressing negativity towards the task. Instead, perceive the task as an occasion to exemplify concentration and channel your efforts. Take, for instance, the scenario where you have a floor that requires cleaning; in this case, direct your entire focus and exertion towards the task of thoroughly cleaning that particular floor. Approach it with humility. It may appear comical, yet it is imperative that you refrain from allowing your mind to stray whilst engaged in this assignment. Devote your complete focus to it. In contemporary times, we have developed a propensity for succumbing to the countless diversions presented by social media, telecommunication devices, and the disruptions that permeate our day-to-day existence. Eliminate all potentialities of this occurrence as you carry out the task. This exercise will assist you in developing your ability to maintain concentration. It is essential to consistently recognize your thoughts and communicate your awareness of them, while promptly redirecting your attention to the task at hand. The more you engage in deliberate practice, the higher your proficiency in this skill will grow.

When observing Buddhist monks engaged in their daily responsibilities, they exhibit an unwavering commitment to remain undisturbed. They diligently perform the allocated tasks, assigning equal significance to each of them. It is advisable to implement this approach within your own personal endeavors, as the absence of humility can perpetuate internal conflict, thereby hindering the optimal efficacy of meditation. In even popular works of literature, such as the acclaimed novel "Eat, Pray, Love" by Elizabeth Gilbert, the author eloquently shares her personal encounter at a retreat, during which she was instructed to engage in meditation or focus her mind on emptiness. Constantly, her mind battled, as it had been ingrained in her since early childhood to react contemplatively to specific stimuli. We are politely requested to exercise caution and consider our words prior to uttering them. We are requested to exercise proper etiquette. Attaining fulfillment through meditation will prove to be a challenging endeavor, far from the easiest venture you will undertake in your life. Nevertheless, when one begins to observe their chakras and acknowledge their respective necessities, the likelihood of being able to engage in meditation and reap its benefits substantially increases.

In the course of your lifetime, you will encounter various obstacles. Nevertheless, upon successfully integrating meditation into your daily existence, you will observe a notable enhancement in your outlook on life's fluctuations, characteristically embracing a more optimistic stance, while concurrently ensuring the unfailing equilibrium of your energy centers, commonly known as chakras. Strive to respond with optimism and cooperation towards those in your vicinity. Exhibit kindness and demonstrate mindfulness of the diverse perspectives through which the world can be perceived. Please be aware that your situation is not unique. Despite being confident in our convictions, demonstrating a modicum of humility can yield significant benefits. It is imperative to grant autonomy to individuals in forming their own opinions regarding matters that impact them, while acknowledging the existence of multiple perspectives that collectively constitute the inherent truth.

An Exposition On The Fundamentals Of The 7 Fundamental Chakras

Chakras serve as pivotal energy centers, and while the general knowledge and literature predominantly recognize seven chakras, it is essential to acknowledge that the human body encompasses a total of 114 chakra points. There exist merely seven fundamental points known as chakras, and these specific ones will be expounded upon in the subsequent chapters. In addition to chakras, there exist energy meridians that govern the circulation of energy throughout the body. These channels are commonly referred to as "nadis." A triangular configuration is established when the convergence of energy from three distinct "nadis" takes place within the body, leading to the recognition of this configuration as a chakra point. Despite the common perception of chakra points as energy spheres, their physical form is actually that of a triangular shape. The diverse attributes exhibited by an individual are a consequence of the efficacy of these chakra centers. Every spiritual trajectory encapsulated within the physical form can be characterized as a voyage commencing at the initial significant hub of energy and culminating at the final one. Furthermore, the remaining five pivotal aspects are addressed. This is an odyssey where energy undergoes transit between dimensions as it traverses from the Root to the Crown locations. Below is a succinct elucidation of the seven primary chakra points, intended to acquaint you with the notion and facilitate comprehension. The initial chakra, referred to as the Root Chakra, resides at the base of the spinal column. It establishes a direct connection to our planet and possesses a distinctive red hue. It is further recognized as Maludhara. The Root Chakra is linked to an individual's capacity for survival. The fundamental essentials that are necessary for human survival, along with the inherent instincts that have ensured our survival from ancient times, are shared by nearly all living beings. Consequently, these aspects possess a universal nature. The collective possession of this instinct among all sentient beings serves to indicate that there exists a significantly broader cosmos in which we merely occupy a fragmentary position. The nexus between mankind and our terrestrial habitat, and our existence on this globe along with the cognizance of our corporeal existence, are likewise linked to the Root. Our sentiment of security and our sense of belonging within this place are both inextricably linked to it. This reaches far beyond surface-level understanding. On a broader and elevated scale, it bestows upon us the feeling of being rooted and comfortable within our immediate surroundings. The hereditary recollections of an individual are transmitted from one generation to another through the root chakra. Many individuals encounter diverse obstacles as a result of these memories, as they frequently can pose barriers. The recollections of warfare, calamities, and other experiential recollections tied to the existence and resilience of an individual on this celestial body are collectively housed within the Root. Individuals with a fully operational Root Chakra exhibit concern for the physical requirements of their bodies. They strive to maintain a strong connection with the natural world, prioritize their dietary choices, and engage in regular physical activity. These individuals exhibit a commendable level of organization and maintain mastery over various facets of their lives. A properly functioning Root chakra establishes a foundation for the harmonious equilibrium of all remaining chakras. It confers upon an individual the vitality and impetus to effectively address the mundane tribulations and exigencies of everyday existence. The Sacral Chakra, also known as the Second Chakra, is situated just above the base and is responsible for governing aspects such as self-worth, sexual expression, artistic inspiration, and feelings of dissatisfaction experienced by an individual. The location of this particular chakra resides in the region between the naval area and pubic bone, with its corresponding elemental association being water. It is accompanied by an orange hue. The second chakra governs the nature of your interpersonal connections, both with individuals within your vicinity and with the larger global community. The sacral chakra holds dominion over the enjoyment derived from one's corporeal existence, emotional well-being, and sexual vitality. It oversees the manner in which you engage with others and regulates their impact on your emotions and behaviors. It facilitates the cultivation of emotional equilibrium by aiding in the management and exploration of one's feelings. Upon birth, an individual begins perceiving the world and continues to accumulate knowledge. Their lack of knowledge pertains to the authenticity of said information. The passage of time consolidates this information into a fixed notion, ultimately influencing his character. In order to appropriately manage that information, it is imperative for the Root and Sacral Chakras to be functioning optimally. Individuals who possess a highly attuned Sacral Chakra are characterized by their exuberant disposition and unwavering commitment to living life to its utmost potential. They emit waves of joy and happiness. They engage in social interactions, displaying a propensity for assisting others while consistently demonstrating the necessary vigor to do so. Frequently, it is perceived to be confined to matters of a sexual nature; however, in truth, it encompasses the engagement of an individual. In addition to sexual intimacy, it can also foster a deep sense of connection with your loved ones, including friends and family members. The intricacies of the energy pertaining to the Sacral chakra are significant. To foster a harmonious social existence and establish a profound connection with the collective, it becomes imperative to maintain equilibrium within this sphere. The third chakra, known as the Solar Plexus chakra, embodies the essence of an individual's inner self. It exercises dominion over his personal attributes, encompassing his determination, eloquence, assertiveness, and aptitude. The level of autonomy displayed by an individual is intricately connected to the Solar Plexus region. This chakra is guided by the principles of power and intellect possessed by an individual. It bears the emblem of fire and exhibits a hue of yellow. It is alternatively referred to as the Naval Chakra. The sense of autonomy or complete absence thereof within one's life is closely associated with the Solar Plexus. It pertains to the manner and location in which you aspire to exist within your life's trajectory. It serves as a catalyst for personal transformation, which ultimately extends its effects outward to the environment. To attain your desired life outcomes, it is imperative to cultivate a stable and balanced Solar Plexus. It reinforces your endeavours by providing a reservoir of resolve and resilience. It not only offers the necessary rigidity to consistently dedicate oneself, but also grants the essential adaptability to alter the path to achievement should any obstacles arise along the chosen course. The Solar Plexus Chakra assumes a vital role in the effective management of one's emotional well-being. It enables individuals to effectively navigate their emotional experiences and express them constructively. When negative feelings and emotions are effectively repressed and unresolved, they manifest as a persistent discomfort and frequently result in undesirable repercussions. When a person has a balanced Solar Plexus, he starts to take pleasure in his challenges. Adversity provides him with amusement and instills in him the determination to overcome. He approaches tasks with an optimistic mindset, which enables him to attain elevated levels of determination and self-control. The notion of honoring one's own individuality is likewise a notable advantage stemming from the equilibrium of the third chakra. You exercise discernment in preventing others from exploiting you, while refraining from exploiting them yourself. Your eventual attainment of success is established upon a strong framework that you meticulously construct through your own efforts. The fourth chakra, known as the Heart Chakra, serves as the pivotal energy center that interconnects the remaining chakras within an individual. There are three chakras located above and below it, and each set is associated with distinct facets of an individual's being. The lower three pertain to the corporeal dimensions of an individual's existence and character, whereas the upper three are more aligned with matters of spirituality, cognition, and sagacity. The Heart Chakra resides in the space that serves as a juncture between these two layers. The purpose of this chakra is to ascribe significance to our encounters encompassing both the material and ethereal realms, such as sensations of discomfort, affection, distress, and empathy. It regulates and maintains them in equilibrium, ensuring that our psychological and physiological well-being remains unimpacted to the point of jeopardizing our safety. There exists a profound connection between mental and physical well-being, a notion which contemporary medical practitioners are currently validating. Emotions of affection and benevolence are linked to the Heart Chakra. These encompass notions of romantic affection, parental devotion, and compassionate sentiments toward one's children, friends, and fellow beings. Demonstrating care for individuals in your vicinity, without any expectation of recompense, also pertains to this matter. In addition to the love of a romantic nature, the universal love for all beings is also influenced by the Heart Chakra. Individuals with a harmoniously aligned Heart Chakra frequently exhibit sincerity, displaying qualities of empathy and genuine concern for others. Their personalities hold no enigmas as they greatly prefer to openly divulge information. They demonstrate a remarkable degree of self-acceptance, and extend the same acceptance to others regardless of their caste, color, or creed, exhibiting a profound inclusivity. The Throat Chakra, belonging to the upper tier of chakras, is designated as the fifth in the series. This aspect pertains to your capacity to effectively communicate your thoughts and ideas to others through various mediums. This pertains to the act of authentically conveying one's true identity to others, and effectively expressing one's thoughts and ideas in their unaltered state. The Throat Chakra functions as the spokesperson for the rest of the chakras. Individuals whose throat chakra is functioning optimally possess the capacity to discern their needs and effectively communicate them to others. Frequently individuals with this characteristic excel in public speaking, teaching, and music due to their adeptness at maintaining composure while effectively articulating their thoughts. It encompasses not only the domains of oral or verbal communication, but also a myriad of methods employed for the purpose of communication. Additionally, it serves as a conduit for the expression of the collective energy of all other chakras. Being a proficient communicator necessitates possessing the ability to listen attentively, as one recognizes the importance of understanding others' perspectives before articulating one's own thoughts in a direct manner. This proficiency enables them to effectively analyze situations and formulate improved decisions with regards to rectifying them. It comes as no surprise, therefore, that they excel as advisors. In a state of affliction and seeking the presence of another individual, an individual is essentially desiring the company of someone who possesses a well-developed Throat Chakra, regardless of their conscious awareness of this fact. This can be attributed to the fact that these individuals possess superior listening skills and possess exceptional advisory capabilities; both of which are highly desirable qualities in a support system during times of significant stress. Several physiological conditions arise when the Throat Chakra deviates from its usual state. Some of the symptoms that may be experienced include frequent episodes of headache, discomfort in the throat, tension in the neck muscles, and a sensation of obstruction in the jaw area. Individuals occasionally engage in deception and harbor considerable concerns regarding trust. One of the consequences includes occasional stammering due to the inability to locate appropriate language. The Sixth Chakra, also known as the Third Eye, is a highly ethereal aspect of an individual's energy system. It pertains to an individual's spiritual, intuitive, and introspective faculties. The object possesses an indigo hue and is situated betwixt the ocular regions. It is alternatively referred to as the Brow Chakra; however, it is more commonly acknowledged and referred to as the Third Eye. The primary emphasis of the Third Eye lies in the acquisition of discerning knowledge that facilitates the soundness of decision-making. When the individual achieves an optimal state, they gain the ability to effectively harness the remaining chakras, enabling them to delve deeper into their inner self. An individual who possesses an equilibrated state of this chakra frequently possesses prescience, whereby their intuition serves as a guiding force, enabling them to be aware of information prior to its verbalization. They possess a robust capacity for envisioning, which enhances their ability to make more insightful judgments that are informed by their practical expertise and intuitive discernment simultaneously. It is of utmost importance for an individual to make decisions in a manner that allows them to remain steadfast in their authenticity, principles, and moral code, and it is at this juncture that the sixth chakra of an individual becomes relevant. This chakra enables one to have transcendent encounters, such as experiencing déjà-vu and possessing clairvoyant abilities. It enables an individual to perceive a broader range of visual and auditory phenomena. The faculties of the human mind become perceptible and comprehensible to an individual upon the activation of their Third Eye. He acquires the capacity to interpret The Third Eye of an individual, enhancing his discernment and intuition, resulting in improved decision-making that is guided by his emotional insights. This expands his perspective and instills in him a mindset that not only engages in critical inquiry, but also embraces acceptance. A well-developed sixth chakra enables an individual to address their challenges with clarity and simplicity. This aids in the alleviation of undesirable stress, whilst affording him the opportunity to select the most straightforward resolution to his predicaments. The seventh chakra, known as the Crown Chakra, pertains to the spiritual and transcendent dimensions of an individual. It oversees the elevated facets of one's character. The essence of an individual and their capacity to engage in introspection within their own being are correlated with the Crown Chakra. The said anatomical location corresponds to the highest point of the cranium and it exhibits a prominent violet hue. This particular energy center enables an individual to experience a sense of unity with the entirety of existence and to comprehend the fundamental and profound interconnectedness between their own being and all other entities. Obtaining permission to access the Crown can prove to be highly intricate for many novices, owing to the diminished emphasis placed on spiritual facets in contemporary society. Throughout previous centuries, the role of religion and its associated practices has been instrumental in the advancement and progression of humanity. Neglecting religion and completely removing it from our lives can have adverse consequences, whereas acknowledging its significance as a means to finding inner peace can aid us in becoming more virtuous individuals for the benefit of those in our vicinity. The connection between the Crown and the soul is profound and intricate, unbreakable even. In established academic domains, the Crown is recognized as both the point of entry for the soul into a physical vessel upon birth and the pathway it follows upon the demise of an individual. The port serves as a conduit not only connecting an individual to his immediate surroundings but also to the global community as a whole. It facilitates the maintenance of a connection with the broader aspects of one's being, enabling communication with them. In prior times, the concept of Chakra, whether individual or collective, was primarily regarded as pertaining to the realm of spirituality. However, contemporary physics has now provided evidence that every individual entity and every material component is essentially comprised of energy at the atomic scale. It has become evident that this inherent energy has perpetually existed within these entities and will persist indefinitely. However, there remains a significant portion of the population that regards it as lacking in scientific credibility. It is anticipated that scientific evidence will be substantiated in the foreseeable future for the Chakra system, potentially leading to its formal recognition as a comprehensive discipline in both medical and artistic domains. Individuals who possess an impeccably functioning Crown Chakra exhibit qualities of altruism and possess an expansive and receptive disposition. They perceive themselves as merely a component of a significantly larger world and regard themselves as one among numerous individuals. It is apparent that individuals of this kind devote themselves to enhancing the wellbeing of both humanity and the natural world. These individuals frequently demonstrate aptitude as advocates seeking to preserve and protect animals, plants, and the environment. Assisting others is inherent to their nature.

Engaging In The Practice Of The Three Lower Chakras

Engaging with the three subordinate chakras facilitates the restoration of equilibrium in the tangible realm. The term 'this plane' pertains to the realm of tangible existence encompassing all the indispensable elements facilitating a prosperous, satisfying life within our current milieu.

Throughout various epochs and periods, societies have encountered their share of challenges. However, our present era is influenced comprehensively, encompassing regions where basic survival necessities like sustenance and potable water are paramount concerns, regions ravaged by the detrimental effects of warfare and humanity's distinctive inclination for discord, and regions brimming with technological marvels so advanced that they bear semblance to the imaginative worlds depicted in works of speculative fiction.

It should be noted that the trio of lower chakras pertains to matters of physical stability, emotional bonds, and self-esteem. In numerous respects, they exhibit resemblances to the foundational tiers outlined in Maslow's hierarchy of needs. Although it is remarkable to encounter accounts of individuals practicing yoga and related disciplines who manage to triumph over cold, hunger, and various forms of deprivation, it remains true that the majority of us are more capable of concentrating on self-improvement when our fundamental necessities are fulfilled. Please be advised that needs should be distinguished from desires, as unmet desires can hinder the process of aesthetic learning.

One could potentially compile extensive volumes detailing methods for stabilizing and harmonizing one's physical existence. However, in the interest of conciseness, this book will concentrate on uncomplicated meditation methods.

Commence by taking a seat in a posture that affords comfort. If you possess adequate adaptability, assume a seated position with your legs crossed or in a half-lotus or full lotus formation. If you are unable to do so due to general stiffness, arthritis, an injury, or any other condition, we recommend sitting in a plain wooden chair with your feet positioned flat on the floor.

Inhale softly, and assume an upright posture. Envision a concentrated sphere of energy situated at the lowermost point of your spinal column. Strive to attain utmost equilibrium in your thoughts. The designated hue for the root chakra is red, reminiscent of the crimson flow coursing within your circulatory system or the rich hue seen in clay.

The elemental association of this particular chakra is earth, and it is traditionally referred to as Muladhara. Envision it as a bountiful expanse, adorned by a majestic, time-honored oak tree in its center. Establish within yourself a cognitive framework of nourishing crimson roots that extend profoundly into the soil. Allow the extensions of that foundational structure to permeate the soil, anchoring you firmly, akin to the roots of a sturdy tree.

When one experiences the sensation of being akin to a venerable oak tree, firmly rooted in a profound bedrock, it is advisable to progress towards the sacral chakra.

The sacral chakra can be found in close proximity to the reproductive organs. It resides in a position superior to the root chakra, yet inferior to the abdominal region. There is a deliberate correlation between the term "sacral" and "sacred." This is due to its proximity to the sacrum, a collection of vertebrae that undergo fusion during late adolescence or early adulthood, thereby constituting the posterior region of the pelvic floor.

It is commonly held that this bone was obtained from animals and presented as an act of sacrifice. If we consider Maslow's hierarchy, it pertains to aspects such as human relationships, sensuality, and love, while also being linked to creativity, innovation, and intuition.

It encompasses the sentiment of unequivocal certainty, or the quivering sensation evoked – akin to fluttering butterflies in the stomach – in anticipation of embarking upon a novel endeavor. It exercises control over one's emotional bonds - a condition that may manifest as desirable or undesirable, as commonly acknowledged.

Consider the types of interpersonal connections that bring you the most satisfaction, those that you are aware promote positivity, compassion, and empathy. Acknowledge the understanding that love occasionally entails the act of asserting oneself by declining – akin to the manner in which one would address a child. Acknowledge that it manifests in diverse manners, and that the most superior ones are accompanied by comprehension.

The hue assigned to this specific chakra manifests as a luxuriant shade of orange – akin to the hue exhibited by day lilies that graciously unfold their blossoms each day, alongside the vibrant tints exhibited by tiger lilies, nasturtiums, and zinnias; indeed, a hue reminiscent of the vivid intensity of a flame. This Chakra is referred to as Svadhishthana.

This particular chakra may require considerable time to achieve harmony, especially if one is in the early stages of life and has not yet established mature relationships. Imagine yourself nestled within the embrace of the venerable oak tree, akin to a cherished infant held tenderly in the loving arms of their parents; visualize yourself tenderly cradling a young child.

Once a sense of stability is perceived, albeit temporary, proceed to address the solar plexus chakra. This constitutes the core essence of your existence. Its hue is a pristine, exquisite yellow, and it bears the name Manipura. It pertains to one's self-esteem, encompassing one's sense of personal value and self-regard. It is supported by both the root and sacral chakras, effectively maintaining their stability and equilibrium.

The prudent application of rational judgment informs us that the charming celebrity who captivates our emotions is unlikely to become a candidate for romantic companionship. It entails being capable of concentrating on a particular talent or skill to successfully realize a creative endeavor.

It permits the restriction of a certain context, enabling one to effectively harness their skills and generate a product. In essence, it denotes a disposition characterized by self-assurance and authority, devoid of arrogance or tyranny.

These are simply abbreviated depictions of these chakras; however, they will provide you with a basic understanding of their interconnected functioning. These three elements establish the groundwork for the subsequent three components.

Conclusion

I wholeheartedly trust that this book has proven beneficial to you and that you have derived significant value from it. This serves as a rudimentary outline of the meditation procedure and the process of restoring balance to the chakras. There exists a multitude of permutations to the procedure, and I highly encourage you to discover the approach that proves efficacious for your circumstances. Moreover, it might be advantageous for you to acquire knowledge about alternative breathing techniques that could prove to be more conducive to your pursuit of equilibrium and the restoration of your chakras.

Temporarily, review the contents of this book and determine the opportune moment to effectuate transformative changes in your life. Henceforth, maintain a reverential stance and cultivate a receptive state wherein your chakras may unfurl and embrace the experiences of your existence. If their functionality is in a state of dormancy or impedes the transmission of energy, engaging in the pursuit of equilibrium and serenity in one's life will prove highly advantageous.

The capacity of your physique to undergo healing is more extensive than what has been conventionally acknowledged.

Thank you for taking the time to peruse this text.

www.ingramcontent.com/pod-product-compliance
Lightning Source LLC
Chambersburg PA
CBHW050029130526
44590CB00042B/2240